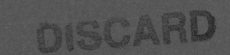

Labor Day

Rebecca Rissman

Heinemann Library
Chicago, Illinois

www.heinemannraintree.com
Visit our website to find out more information about Heinemann-Raintree books.

To order:
☎ Phone 888-454-2279
💻 Visit www.heinemannraintree.com to browse our catalog and order online.

Edited by Adrian Vigliano and Rebecca Rissman
Designed by Ryan Frieson
Picture research by Tracy Cummins
Leveling by Nancy E. Harris
Originated by Capstone Global Library Ltd.
Printed in China by South China Printing Company Ltd.

15 14 13 12 11 10
10 9 8 7 6 5 4 3 2 1

Library of Congress Cataloging-in-Publication Data
Rissman, Rebecca.
  Labor Day / Rebecca Rissman.
    p. cm.—(Holidays and festivals)
  Includes bibliographical references and index.
  ISBN 978-1-4329-4062-1 (hc)—ISBN 978-1-4329-4081-2 (pb) 1. Labor Day—Juvenile literature. I. Title.
HD7791.R55 2011
394.264—dc22
                                  2009052873

Acknowledgments

The author and publishers are grateful to the following for permission to reproduce copyright material: AP Photo/John Heller **pp.17, 23 bottom**; AP Photo/Carlos Osorio **p.20**; Corbis ©Astock **p.5**; Corbis ©Bettmann **pp.9, 8**; Getty Images/Lambert Studios **p.12**; Getty Images/Jupiterimages **p.18**; Getty Images/Colorblind **p.19**; Getty Images/Ken Fisher **p.21**; istockphoto ©John Clines **p.22**; Library of Congress Prints and Photographs Division **pp.6, 7, 10, 23 center, 23 top**; Library of Congress Prints and Photographs Division/Lewis W. Hine **p.11**; Photolibrary/Imagesource Imagesource **p.16**; Shutterstock ©Monkey Business Images **p.4**; Shutterstock ©Galina Barskaya **p.14**; Shutterstock ©Orange Line Media **p.15**; The Granger Collection, New York **p.13**.

Cover photograph of a group of professionals reproduced with permission of Corbis/image100. Back cover photograph reproduced with permission of Library of Congress Prints and Photographs Division.

Every effort has been made to contact copyright holders of any material reproduced in this book. Any omissions will be rectified in subsequent printings if notice is given to the publisher.

Contents

What Is a Holiday?

People celebrate holidays.
A holiday is a special day.

Labor Day is a holiday.
Labor Day is in September.

The Story of Labor Day

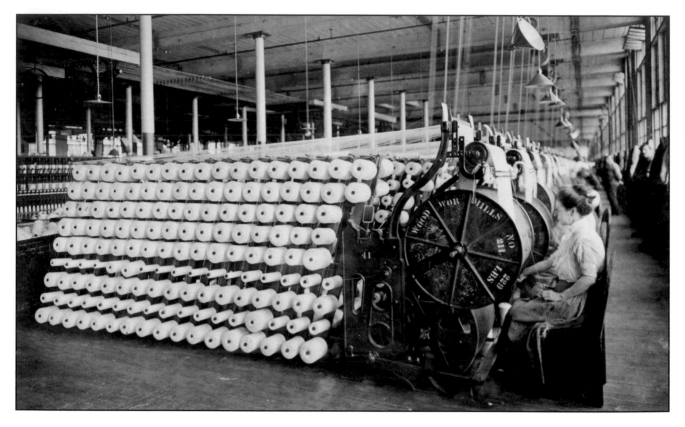

Long ago many people worked in factories. Factories are buildings filled with machines and workers.

People made many things in factories.
But factories were dangerous.

People could get hurt working in factories. People did not earn very much money.

Factory workers needed to stand up for themselves.

They started to form labor unions. Labor unions are groups of workers that stand up for their rights.

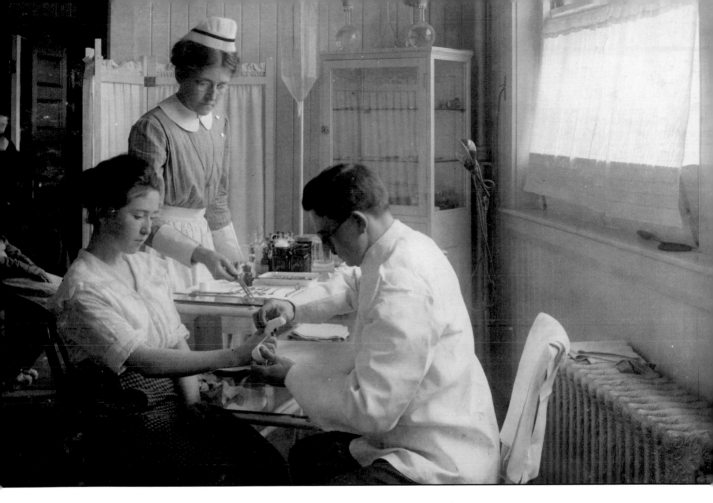

These labor unions helped workers make more money. Labor unions helped workers stay safe at work.

 Peter Maguire was a union leader. He wanted a day to be thankful for America's workers.

In 1882, America celebrated the first Labor Day.

Celebrating Labor Day

On Labor Day most schools and businesses are closed.

People spend time with family and friends.

People spend time outdoors.

People watch parades.

People eat picnics together.

And people are grateful for all of
America's workers.

Labor Day Symbols

Labor unions are symbols of Labor Day.

America's workers are symbols of Labor Day.

Calendar

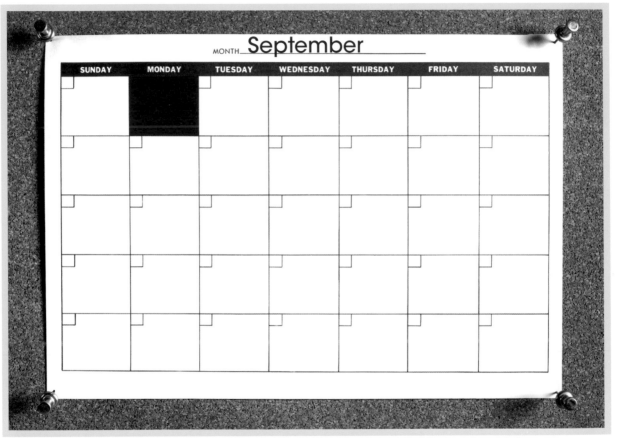

MONTH **September**

SUNDAY	MONDAY	TUESDAY	WEDNESDAY	THURSDAY	FRIDAY	SATURDAY

 Labor Day is the first Monday in September.

Picture Glossary

factory a big building where many people work. Some factories have many machines inside.

labor union a group of workers that stand up for their rights

parade a group of people marching together to celebrate something

Index

Note to Parents and Teachers

Before reading
Explain that every September, Americans celebrate Labor Day. Ask if the children can guess what we are celebrating on Labor Day. Ask for impressions about work: can they name many types of jobs? What do the children want to be when they become adults? What kind of work do they already participate in?

After reading
Plan a field trip to a local factory or workplace. Make sure the children get to interact with a diverse segment of workers representing a wide array of different skills and responsibilities. Encourage questions!